Chant
Made
Simple

ROBERT M. FOWELLS

PA...

BREWSTER, MASSACHUSETTS

1000 Bt 8.95

Library of Congress Cataloging-in-Publication Data

Fowells, Robert M., 1921–
    Chant made simple / Robert M. Fowells.
        p. cm.
    ISBN 1-55725-253-X (pbk.)
        1. Chants (Plain, Gregorian, etc.)—Instruction and study. I. Title.
    MT860 .F58 2000
    782.32'22—dc21   00-032692

Unless otherwise designated, scripture quotations are taken from the King James Version of the Bible.

The Gregorian Chant pieces, excerpted from the *Graduale Triplex*, have been reproduced with the permission of S.A. La Froidfontaine, 72300 Solesmes, France.

10 9 8 7 6 5 4 3 2 1

© 2000 by Robert M. Fowells
1-55725-253-X

Published by Paraclete Press
Brewster, Massachusetts
www.paracletepress.com
Printed in the United States of America.

Contents

Introduction

Gregorian chant is the earliest music that we can transcribe accurately. Its first notation dates back to the ninth century. Unhappily, most Catholic churches no longer sing it because it is in Latin, and no Protestant churches sing it because it sounds Catholic. But the chant is the sound that carried the Christian message for 1500 years before there even were any Protestants. Perhaps in the new millennium we might all be grateful enough for the last 2000 years that any church could include an appropriate excerpt of chant in its service, sung in the original Latin, with the biblical translation in the bulletin.

This collection contains simple chants based on biblical quotations which should be useful to the following:

- Any church that would like an occasional connection with the whole church's history.

- Early music lovers who would like to perform the "earliest of the early."
- Choral music directors who could use the open vowels and short ranges for both warm-ups and performance.
- Anyone who would like a simple introduction to the latest understanding of medieval chant performance.

Being brought up a Presbyterian (a Scottish Huguenot!), this author had never heard chant until Gustave Reese played some 78 rpm recordings in graduate school. Hearing the seemingly formless melodies move like a swallow enjoying the summer breezes started a lifelong fascination. Some thirty years later, at my invitation, Dom Jean Claire, chantmaster at the abbey of Saint-Pierre de Solesmes in France, taught chant for a month at California State University, Los Angeles. His combination of brilliance, humility, and gentle humor so fascinated the students that one of them, obviously unaware of Catholic protocol, asked if he was an ordinary priest or a saint!

Since he could not return, Dom Claire suggested that we invite M. Clément Morin, P.S.S., a Sulpician priest, director of the Grand Seminary choir and retired dean of music at the University of Montréal. From his very first lecture M. Morin opened a whole new concept of chant interpretation, one that showed that the chant was not an unimaginative mantra, as many thought it was, but a series of "little musical words" that adorned the text, in true medieval fashion, with signs for phrasing in its notation and often little themes that seemed descriptive. These discoveries not only gave the chant a new sound but gave us a closer relationship with our ancestors of the Middle Ages.

Melodic Notation

THE SQUARE NOTATION USED TODAY is a small version of the notation used in the twelfth century for manuscripts large enough that the whole choir could read from them. Once you are used to square notation, it is much easier to read than newer note-head editions because the designs are so obvious above the syllables to which they apply. If you look at the first example of square notation, found on page 17 of this book, you will notice that there are signs above and below the staff. These neumes from our earliest notation will be discussed in the next chapter, although we do not need them for determining the melodies.

Since most chants have a very short range, only four lines are used. There are two clefs, a C-clef (𝄴) and an F-clef (𝄵). Their function is only to designate the line that has a half-step below it, since the pitch level to be sung is entirely a matter of ease for the singers. The staffs are moveable so that the melody will fit on the four lines, in most cases, without ledger lines.

The notes move in an obvious order except in two instances. A two-note neume, low to high, is written with the low note on the bottom and the higher note directly above it (⊥). The three-note porrectus, high–low–high, looks like some kind of a slide (⩘) but was merely a matter of convenience so that the copyist did not have to lift his square-tipped pen from the page. The top of the slide is the first note, the bottom is the second, and the third note is directly above the bottom note. Some notes are diamond shaped instead of square, another matter of ease for the copyist which has nothing to do with the length of the sound.

Some notes, called "liquescent," are warnings of the need for careful diction in medieval accoustics. They are shown in the square notation as tiny notes, instead of regular-sized notes, on the end of the neumes, and they appear where two vowels have no protective consonant between them or where two neighboring consonants need time to be pronounced distinctly.

Another note that differs is the quilisma (⩗).

It appears in the oldest manuscripts as the addition of a half-step into the old pentatonic scale—c–d–f–g–a which became c–d–e–f–g–a. Because of the startling sound of the half-step, the old sign for a question mark was used as a warning to sing lightly.

Only one accidental is used in chant, a b-flat (♭), which lasts only for the word in which it occurs. Chant pitch of course is only relative and does not denote an exact level such as 435, 440, etc.

Chant melodies are not built on major and minor scales but on the medieval modes, each with its own final and dominant tones, the dominant being the reciting tone that would be used if the chant were a simple intonation. Melodies with odd-numbered modes (authentic) lie mostly above the final, and those with the even-numbered modes (plagal) lie lower, often below the final. Knowing these two structural pitches can often help in deciding which note of a neume is most important. They are listed beneath each of the chants in the later portion of this book.

Following these pitches through a melody often reveals how the chant was ornamented. For instance, the first chant in this book, *Dominus dixit*, obviously ornaments a minor third, d–f. The second one, *In splendoribus*, begins and ends with an ornamented minor third, d–f, but brightens up in the middle with a major third, f–a.

MODERN	BASIC	LENGTHENED
		(second note), (both notes)
		(both notes)
		(last note), (last two notes), (all notes)
		(last note), (first two notes)
		(first note), (last note), (all notes)
		(first note), (all notes)
		(first two notes), (all notes)
		(first two notes)
		Three regular notes with the middle one leaning into the last one.

Rhythm

CHANT RHYTHM HAS BEEN A PROBLEM ever since its restoration by the monks of Saint-Pierre de Solesmes over a hundred years ago. Medieval writers, who left us many treatises discussing melodic details, saw no need to discuss anything that was so obvious to them as the rhythm; several centuries had to pass before a system of rhythmic notation was devised for new part-music. The system used for chant rhythm in the first half of the twentieth century was devised by Dom André Mocquereau of Solesmes. In it, every note had the same value except those that he marked with a dot (doubled) or an overhead line (lengthened). His rhythmic solution plus his aesthetic descriptions of chant phrasing, fully described in the *Liber Usualis*, gave it the beauty for which it has been revered. (The chants used in this book, reprinted from Solesmes' newest edition, the *Graduale Triplex*, still have his signs for those who prefer to sing by the earlier method.)

However, music historians have always known that this rhythmic system had no historical basis. The very first Western music notation was devised by Charlemagne's monks to aid in his desire to unify the church service throughout his empire. Since most of the monks at that time were illiterate and learned both their texts and melodies by rote, they needed the chantmaster's hand to remind them of melodic designs. The original signs, seen above and below the melodies in this book, were only reminders to the chantmaster as to the direction of the melodies, but they did not designate exact pitch. These old neumes did, however, give distinct reminders of longer and shorter notes and even some directions for expression. One of Mocquereau's last students, Dom Eugène Cardine, undertook an exhaustive analysis of these old neumes and revised the concept of chant rhythm. This updated system, described in detail in his treatise *Gregorian Semiology*, is now the basis for a more historically correct performance.

The musical examples from the *Graduale Triplex* which are used here have the old neumes from the Laon Manuscript above the square notes and those from the St. Gall school below. The two almost always agree, so for the sake of simplicity and convenience only the St. Gall neumes are discussed here. Below are some basic principles regarding rhythm, as put forth in Dom Cardine's *Gregorian Semiology*. Those who want a complete description should read his book.

1. Chant has no regular beat but moves in a conversational rhythm. When there is only one note per syllable the chant moves as if it were being read—just as a modern congregation recites the Lord's Prayer in unison without a conductor.

2. When there is more than one note per syllable, the notes move somewhat faster as a simple melodic, somewhat ornamental design.

3. The letter *c* (*celeriter*: faster) designates notes, or groups of

notes, that must be sung more lightly and shortened. (The former system ignores these signs completely.)

4. There are distinct signs for lengthening the notes. Sometimes there is simply a *t* (*tenete*: hold) or just the top of a *t* on a neume (⌐). Another way to show lengthening was to make a more deliberate design, which forced the copyist to slow down his pen (♪⌐♪ ♩ or ♪♩ ♪). A special discovery was the "neumatic break," or "caesura." This break occurred when the scribe interrupted a design that could have been done in one stroke and made two neumes instead (♩ = ♩♩). In this case the note before the break is the more important note in the neume, due to the time it took the copyist to lift the pen and start over. This discovery was especially important for long, ornamental melismas, or chant "cadenzas," because it separated a seemingly formless string of notes into smaller melodic patterns.

Obviously, a system that relies on "shorter or longer" rather than "half or double" makes it impossible for a group to sight-read the music as they normally would. We must remember that the chant was never a dance but an ornamented reading of the Scripture, a beauty that went along with the designs on the cathedrals and the priests' robes. The director must decide what makes the design move best and teach it to the group phrase by phrase. Only sight-reading the square notes can cause rhythmic problems that are hard to eradicate. Just as in the Middle Ages, today's singers easily follow the director's hand as it reminds them of the motion they have been learning.

The previous chart gives the meanings of the most basic neumes that appear in this edition. Then, in the following examples the neumes shown above the Latin words and their translation, across the page from the music, are the ones that effect the normal, conversational flow of the chant.

Some syllables have signs for a series of notes at the same pitch. Under the former system these were considered to be held for the number of notes involved. We now know that these notes were expected to be lightly repercussed, allowing the voice to rise and fall in volume on each note but not to break between notes. In medieval acoustics this would have eliminated the build-up of acoustical delay while giving the impression of a sustained pitch. The neumes vary from light to heavy in the following order, (*•• *)* // *TT*) If the final dot has a *tenete*, it is a sign to lengthen it a bit and to make it lean into the following neume (*•••*).

Symbolism

THE BEGINNING OF "DESCRIPTIVE" music is usually attributed to the late sixteenth-century Italians. It flourished in their madrigals and has become an accepted technique available to all composers ever since. Because Albert Schweitzer was both a biblical and a musical scholar, he exposed all sorts of musical symbolism that Bach used, to add a counterpoint of biblical suggestion to his music.

Only a few medieval music scholars feel that medieval composers, limited to the use of six-note modes with melodies that rarely exceeded an octave, had any symbolic intentions in their compositions. Most of the chants were being sung in one state of development or another long before they were notated, and we have no exact knowledge as to who was responsible for the final version or what ideas they had in mind. But because M. Morin is both a biblical and a musical scholar, some of his concepts of descriptive symbolism are included with the performance suggestions for the chants included here.

Aside from the pictorial patterns, there are four little melodies, "leitmotifs," which happen often enough in significant places that they must have been deliberate. The shortest is fa–mi (f–e), the same notes that the Italian madrigalists used to describe a sigh ("ohime"—alas) which can denote sadness or despair. The theme fa–la–sol (f–a–g) is often used to express joy and an enlarged version, fa–sol–la–sol–la (f–g–a–g–a) expresses "rejoice," as it does in the first theme of the melisma that begins the "Ave Maria" in Advent. Even more intriguing is the use of fa–mi–sol–la (f–e–g–a) as a reminder of the sadness of the cross (fa–mi) and the joy of the Resurrection (sol–la).

Even if we cannot know for certain what the original intentions were, these themes can add a touching counterpoint of thought as we sing the text.

Latin Pronunciation

LATIN IS SIMPLE TO PRONOUNCE BECAUSE it is completely pho-
netic. However, liturgical Latin is softer and more like Italian than
the harder pronunciation taught with scholarly Latin.

VOWELS

A = father
E = men
I = feet
O = for
AE = men
OE = men

Any other combined vowels are both pronounced. If they
occur on a melisma, the second vowel is sung only on the last note.

U after Q or NG and followed by another vowel is sung as a W with the vowel that follows as one syllable, as in Quaint, linguist.

SPECIAL CONSONANTS

C =   K, except
      C before E, AE, OE, I, or Y is like church.
      CC before the same vowels is T-CH,
          with the T ending the previous vowel.
      SC before the same vowels is shall.

CH = K

G =   before A, O, and U is pronouced gun.

G =   before E, I, AE, OE is pronounced judge.

GN = NY (no G sound), like the Italian word gnocci.

H =   silent except in *nihil* and *mihi* when it is k.

J =   Y as in you.

R =   done with a flip of the end of the
          tongue—never attached to the vowel
          before it.

S =   see

TI = Patsy except after S, X, or T when the T
      is regular as in English.

TH = Thomas

X =   ks

XC = ksh before e, ae, oe, i, or y

Z =   dz.

All other consonants are as in English.

Learning the Chant

BECAUSE CHANT IS AN ORNAMENTED reading of the Scripture without bar lines or even distinct beats, it cannot be learned or conducted in the same way as regular choral music. Whether you are learning the chant for yourself before you conduct it, or if you are teaching it to a choir, approach it in the following order:

1. Read the text, being careful to put the accents (underlined) on the proper syllables. Regardless of the ornaments, the words must be pronounced properly.

2. Never just sight-read the chant. The square notes tell only pitch, and a monotonous introduction can lead to rhythmic problems that can be hard to undo.

3. Learn the melodic signs by single words or phrases: Dominus———dixit ad me———Filius meus———es tu. Notes on unaccented syllables should flow towards the accented syllable, and the following ones should fall away. If there is more than one note on the accented syllable, the most important note is probably

the last one unless there is a tenete (➤) on a previous one.

4. Remember that medieval singers learned by rote. Each word and phrase has its own melodic design—M. Morin's "little musical words." Do not sing the whole chant until all of the "words" are learned.

5. In the beginning, conduct with your hand as if you were drawing the design in the air, i.e., higher (➹), low–high (♪), high–low (⋀), low–high–low (↻), etc. At first your singers will get their speed and rhythm from the movement of your hand. Once they are familiar with the design they will need less reminder, and you can simply indicate the rise and fall of the phrases.

CHANTS

Dominus dixit

Graduale Triplex–41 (Christmas Eve)

Do-mi-nus di-xit ad me: Fi-li-us me-us es tu.
Lord said to me: Son my are you.

E-go ho-di-e ge-nu-i te.
I today begot you.

The prevalence of light notes ( ) reminds us that this text is being spoken by God's newborn Son, and therefore should be sung lightly.

The notes on *filius*—three notes, two notes, one note—are a reminder of the Trinity.

The only lengthened notes in the entire chant, on *meus* ( ), are a token of God's pride in his new Son.

Notice that *Dominus* and *ego* are the same person and the same melody.

Mode II: d–f

Psalm 2:7 The LORD said to me, thou art my Son; this day have I begotten thee.

Ps. 2, 7. ℣. 1. 2. 8

DO- MI- NUS * di- xit ad me :
Fí- li- us me- us es tu, e-
go ho- di- e ge- nu- i te.

In splendoribus

Graduale Triplex–44   Christmas Eve

In splen-<u>do</u>-ri-bus sanc-<u>to</u>-rum, ex <u>u</u>-te-ro <u>an</u>-te lu-<u>ci</u>-fe-rum
In   beauties   of holiness,   from womb before   daystar

<u>ge</u>-nu-i   te.
I have begotten you.

In this text, God is speaking. It begins with a low voice inton-
ing minor thirds, and most of the neumes indicate lengthening or
emphasis to give them importance (┌ // ⅄ s).

To be sure we don't drag, we are reminded not to hold on to
light syllables (c).

(1) A longer note (⟋) plus two regular and two longer notes
(⌣).
(2) A longer note (⟋) plus a repercussion followed by the top
note (⌐).
(3) A longer note (⟋) followed by the salicus (⸜). The shining
of the daystar is shown by the highest note in the chant on top
of this neume on *luciferum.*

Mode VI: f–a

Psalm 110 (109):3b   In the brightness of the saints, from the womb before the day star I begot thee. (Douay-Rheims)

CO. VI
RBCKS

IN splendó- ri-bus sanctó- rúm,* éx ú- te- ro án-te lú- cí- fe-rum ✛ gé- nu- i té.

Ps. 109, 3

Ecce virgo

Graduale Triplex–37   (Advent)

Ec-ce vir-go con-<u>ci</u>-pi-et, et <u>pa</u>-ri-et <u>fi</u>-li-um; et
Behold virgin conceive and bear son and

vo-<u>ca</u>-bi-tur <u>no</u>-men <u>e</u>-ius Em-<u>ma</u>-nu-el.
call name his Emmanuel.

(1) One longer note plus three regular ones (♩♫).
(2) Three longer notes (♩♩♩) plus three regular ones (♫).
(3) One longer note followed by the quilisma and two regular notes (♩♫).
(4) Four longer notes (♫).
(5) One longer note (♩) followed by the quilisma and three regular notes (♫).
(6) Two longer notes (♩) followed by three regular notes (♫).
(7) Three notes with the quilisma (♫) followed by two regular notes (♫), the first leaning towards the last one.

Mode I: d–a

Isaiah 7:14   Behold, a virgin shall conceive, and bear a son, and shall call his name Immanuel.

Ecce virgo concipiet, et pariet filium: et vocabitur nomen eius Emmanuel. T. P. Alleluia.

Exsulta filia Sion

Graduale Triplex–47 (Christmas Morning)

Ex-<u>sul</u>-ta <u>fi</u>-li-a <u>Si</u>-on, <u>lau</u>-da <u>fi</u>-li-a le-<u>ru</u>-sa-lem: <u>e</u>-cce Rex
Rejoice daughter Zion shout daughter Jerusalem: behold king

<u>tu</u>-us <u>ve</u>-nit <u>sanc</u>-tus, et Sal-<u>va</u>-tor <u>mun</u>-di.
your comes holy and savior of world.

(1) Four notes with a quilisma, all marked "moderately fast".

(2) The two top notes longer and repercussed.

(3) Two longer notes (✓) and three shorter notes (·./).

(4) Two longer notes plus the quilisma ( ) leading to the top note.

Mode IV: e–a

Zechariah 9:9   Rejoice greatly, O daughter of Zion; shout, O daughter of Jerusalem: behold, thy King cometh unto thee: he is just, and having salvation.

CO. IV
RBCKS

E X-súlta * fí- li- a Si- on, lauda fí- li- a Ie-

rú- sa- lem : ecce Rex tu- us ve- nit sanctus, et Sal-

vá- tor mun- di.

Puer natus est

Graduale Triplex–47 (Christmas Day)

✓   c   c   c   (1)   ⌐
Pu -er na-tus est no- bis, et fi -li-us da-tus est no-bis:
Boy   born   is   to us: and son   given is   to us

            ✓   ⋰   ⊼   (2)   c
cu-ius im-pe-ri-um su-per hu-me-rum e - ius: et vo-ca-bi-tur
whose   kingdom   upon   shoulder   his: and will be called

      (3)   ✓   „⊼   ✓   ⌐
no-men e-ius, ma-gni con-si-li-i An-ge-lus.
name   his   great counsel   angels.

The opening leap of a fifth with its sign for emphasis (✓) is often thought of as a symbol of hands lifting up an offering. The second leap of a fifth on *et* has the sign to move quickly (c) as opposed to the first leap.

The word *filius* is interesting in that it could describe the descending Son, and it also uses the three–two–one figure of the Trinity.

(1) One lengthened note (⌐) followed by a regular repercussion and the higher note. (✓).

On *imperium*, the height of the kingdom is shown by the highest note in the entire chant, with emphasis on the two highest notes (⋰). The *c* on the next syllable reminds us to get moving again. The word also begins with the motif fa–mi–so–la (here transposed to do–ti–re–mi in mode VII), a reminder of the Cross and Glory.

(2) *Eius* is set with a common cadence figure—two long notes (⊼), a five-note ornamental figure with a *c* (∿) and two more lengthened notes (⊼), bringing the phrase to a rest.

The fa–la–sol motif (here transposed to do–mi–re) on *vocabitur* and again on *magni* is a reminder of joy.

(3) The phrase ends with another *eius*, a similar figure with only three ornamental notes in the middle.

Notice the emphasis put on *magni*.

Mode VII: g–d

Isaiah 9:6 For unto us a child is born, unto us a son is given: and the govern-
ment shall be upon his shoulder: and his name shall be called Wonderful,
Counsellor. . . .

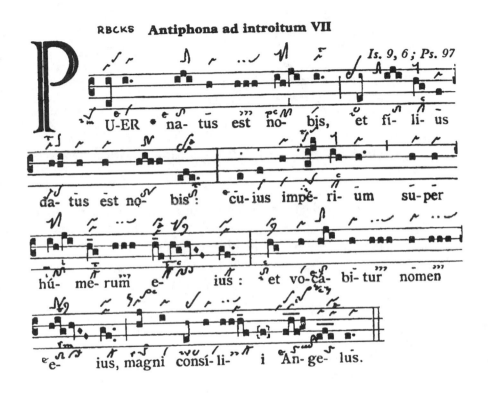

RBCKS **Antiphona ad introitum VII**

Is. 9, 6; Ps. 97

P U-ER * na- tus est no- bis, et fi- li- us

da- tus est no- bis: cu- ius impe- ri- um su- per

hu- me- rum e- ius : et vo-ca- bi- tur nomen

e- ius, magni consi- li- i An- ge- lus.

Vidimus stellam

Graduale Triplex–59 Epiphany

Vi- di - mus stel -lam e-ius in O-ri-en-te, et ve-ni-mus
We have seen   star   his in   east,   and come

cum mu-ne-ri-bus a-do-ra-re Do-mi-num.
with   gifts   to worship   Lord.

Notice that *vidimus* is set with four triplets with a neumatic break between the last two (♫♪).

(1) The notes on the last three syllables of *muneribus* are the common cadence figure, two long, three short, two long (♪·♪♫), resembling ♫ ♫ ♫ .

(2) *Adorare* is given special emphasis by the *x* (*expectare*—wait) and the final cadence figure with a tenete (lilt?) on the second note (♪··♪).

Mode IV: e–a

Matthew 2:2 For we have seen his star in the east, and are come to worship him.

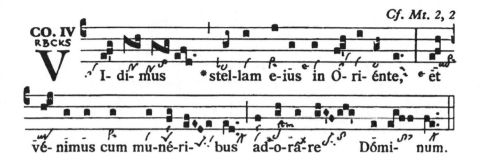

Cf. Mt. 2, 2

CO. IV
RBCKS

VĬ-di-mus *stel-lam e-iūs in Ŏ-ri-ēnte, et vé-nimus cum mu-né-ri-bus ad-o-rā-re Dŏmi-num.

Laetare Ierusalem

Graduale Triplex–108　(Lent)

(1) 𝈀　　　　　　　　　　　𝈀　　　𝈀 (2)　　　(3)
Lae-ta-re le-ru-sa-lem: et　con-ven-tum　fa-ci-te　om-nes
Rejoice　　Jerusalem,　and　　gathering　　make　　all

　　　　　　(4) (5)　　　　　　　　　　　　　　　↗
qui di-li -gi-tis e-am: gaude-te cum lae-ti-ti-a qui in tri-sti-ti-a
who　prize　　her:　rejoice　with　gladness　who in　sadness

(6) (7) 𝈀　　　　　　𝈀　　　　　(8) 𝈀　　　 c //
fu-i-stis: ut ex-sul-te-tis, et sa-ti-e-mi-ni ab u-be-ri-bus
were:　so　　exult　　and　be satisfied　at　　breasts

　　　　　　(9) (10) (11)　𝈀
con-so-la-ti-o-nis vest-rae.
consoling　　　you.

(1) Two regular notes plus two longer (⸱).

(2) Three light notes (⸱⸱) leading into three longer (⸱).

(3) Last three notes longer (⸱)

(4) Four heavy notes (⸱), a quilisma leading into a tenete (⸱)
     (lilt?) followed by two light notes (⸱).

(5) Two light notes, a tenete (lilt?) and two light notes (⸱).

(6) All light (⸱).

(7) Two heavy (𝈀) plus four ornamental (⸱).

(8) Three heavy (⸱) and three light (⸱).

(9) One longer (⸱), two light (⸱), and two longer (⸱).

(10) Two normal plus two longer (⸱), quilisma into a tenete
     (⸱), and two light (⸱).

(11) Two light into the tenete (lilt) followed by three light. (⸱)

Mode V: f–c

Isaiah: 66:10,11   Rejoice ye with Jerusalem, and be glad with her, all ye that love her: rejoice for joy with her, all ye that mourn for her . . . and be satisfied with the breasts of her consolations.

Hosanna filio David

Graduale Triplex–137   (Palm Sunday)

(1)   𝒮   𝐼 c   ↗
Ho-<u>san</u>-na fi-li-o <u>Da</u>-vid: be-ne-<u>dic</u>-tus qui <u>ve</u>-nit in <u>no</u>-mi-ne
Hosanna   to son David: blessed   who comes in   name

(2) ↗   (3)
<u>Do</u>-mi-ni. Rex <u>Is</u>-ra-el: Ho-<u>san</u>-na in ex<u>cel</u>-sis.
of Lord.   King Israel: Hosanna   in   highest.

(1) Wide intervals should always be deliberate. The liquescent top note separating the two *n*'s accentuates the top notes.

(2) A standard cadence figure: two light notes leading to a longer top note (⸽), followed by three light notes (·⟋) which lead into the final syllable (↗).

(3) The square-note neume chosen for the official edition leaves out a note specified by St. Gall. It can be sung as d–e–c–b–a (𝒮·).

Mode VII: g–d

Matthew 21:9 Hosanna to the Son of David: Blessed is he that cometh in the name of the Lord; Hosanna in the highest.

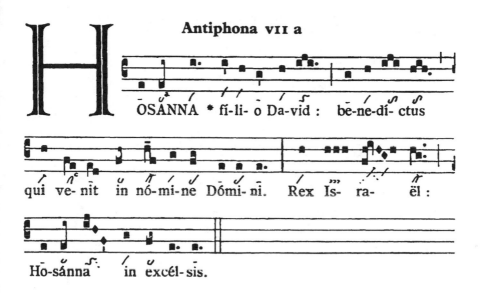

Christus factus est

Graduale Triplex–148   (Palm Sunday)

(1)   (2)   (3) C 𝄾 (4)   (5)
Chri-stus fac-tus est pro no-bis ob-e-di ens us-que ad
Christ   made   was for us   obedient   all the way to

 ⌐   (6)   ⌐⌐ (7) (8) (9)
mor-tem, mor-tem au-tem cru-cis.
death,   death   even   on cross.

(1) One longer note repercussed to the second note at the same pitch
(⌐⌐).

(2) Two regular notes plus three longer ones (⌐) followed by four longer
ones (⌐⌐).

(3) Four shorter notes, (⌐), two longer notes (⌐⌐), and three regular
notes (⌐).

(4) One longer note (⌐), two shorter notes, and one longer note (⌐).

(5) Two regular notes plus three shorter ones (⌐⌐).

(6) One longer note (⌐) followed by the salicus which begins with the
repercussion (⌐).

(7) Two longer notes (⌐), a quilisma followed by two longer notes
(⌐), followed by another quilisma with a lengthened top note (⌐),
and two short notes (⌐) leading into the next word.

(8) Three heavily repercussed notes followed by a long clivis (⌐⌐⌐).
This is often described as a reminder of the nails being driven into the
cross.

(9) *l.* long melisma following *crucis*, with two short notes and three
longer ones (⌐), a salicus (⌐), and a common cadence figure which
looks deceptive in the square notation. It should be performed as
⌐⌐⌐⌐⌐ .

This melisma also contains two motives which relate to the cruci-
fiction. The pattern f–e–g–a (fa–mi–sol–la) is a reminder of the death
(fa–mi) and resurrection (sol–la) and the pattern f–a–g–a
(fa–la–sol–la) represents the joy of the resurrection.

Mode V: f–c

Philippians 2:8 And being found . . . as a man, he humbled himself and became obedient unto death, even the death of the cross.

Hoc corpus

Graduale Triplex–170   (Holy Week)

✓ c   ✓ ⌐ (1) ⌐   ⌐
Hoc <u>cor</u>-pus, quod pro <u>vo</u>-bis tra-<u>de</u>-tur: hic <u>ca</u>-lix <u>no</u>-vi
This   body   which for   you   is broken   this cup   new

(2) ⌐ c   ⌐ ⌐   ⌐
tes-ta-<u>men</u>-ti est in <u>me</u>-o <u>san</u>-gui-ne, <u>di</u>-cit <u>Do</u>-mi-nus;
testament   is in   my   blood   said   Lord

⌐   (3)   ⌐   (4)
hoc <u>fa</u>-ci-te, quo-ti-es-<u>cum</u>-que <u>su</u>-mi-tis, in <u>me</u>-am
this   do   as often as you   drink   in   my

c   ⌐
com-me-mo-ra-ti-<u>o</u>-nem.
       memory.

(1) One longer (↗) plus three light (⁄.).
(2) Two regular notes plus three longer (⌐⌐⁄).
(3) Two light notes (⁚) plus three longer (⌐⌐).
(4) One longer note (⌐), two light (⁚), and three longer
(⌐⌐).

Mode VIII: g–c

CHANT MADE SIMPLE

1 Corinthians 11:24, 25   This is my body which is broken for you. . . . This cup is the new testament in my blood: this do ye, as oft as ye drink it, in remembrance of me.

Resurrexi

Graduale Triplex–196 (Easter)

S   (1)   **π**   **ππ**   (2)

Re-sur-<u>re</u>-xi, et <u>ad</u>-huc <u>te</u>-cum sum, al-le-<u>lu</u>-ia: Po-su-<u>i</u>-sti
I am risen   and   now   with you am: You   put

λ,,   *√:*   (3)   C   **⊸**   (4)   **λ̄**

su- per me <u>ma</u>-num <u>tu</u>-am, al-le-<u>lu</u>-ia. Mi-<u>ra</u>-bi-lis <u>fac</u>-ta est
on   me   hand   your.   Wonderfully   shown   is

(5)   (6) (7)   **π**

sci-<u>en</u>-ti-a <u>tu</u>-a, al-le-<u>lu</u>-ia, al-le-<u>lu</u>-ia.
knowledge   your.

(1) One longer note (⌐) followed by three repercussed notes
     (,,,) leading into the next syllable.
(2) A special torculus (♪). Only the last two notes are length-
     ened.
(3) A longer note (⊸), three medium light notes (,') and a
     final longer note (⊸).
(4) Two longer notes (√) and three light ones (·.⁄).
(5) A longer note followed by the quilisma (⌐ᴡ).
(6) First note longer (⌐ᴡ).
(7) First note longer, followed by three repercussed notes leading
     into the next syllable (⌐,,).

Mode IV: e–g

*Psalm 139 (138): 18,5,6   When I awake, I am still with thee. Thou hast . . .
laid thine hand upon me. Such knowledge is too wonderful for me.*

Pascha nostrum

Graduale Triplex–199 (Easter)

(1) ✓ (2) (3)
Pas-cha **nos**-trum im-mo-**la**-tus est **Chri**-stus, al-le-**lui**a.
Paschal lamb   our   sacrificed   is   Christ

c (4)   (5)   C
I-ta-que e-pu-**le**-mur in **a**-zy-mis   sin-ce-ri-**ta**-tis
Therefore   let us feast   on unleavened bread's   sincerity

(6) (7) (8) (9) C
et **ve**-ri-**ta**-tis, al-le-**lu**-ia, al-le-**lu**-ia, al-le-**lu**-ia.
and   truth.

(1) Two longer notes (⨯) followed by a quilisma leading to two longer
     notes (⤳⨯).

(2) Three longer notes (⟋) followed by a four-note ornament
     (⤳✔) leading into *est*.

(3) A four-note ornament expressing joy —fa–la–sol–fa.

(4) Two longer notes (⌐⌐), three shorter notes (⟋), a three-note fig-
     ure with the top notes as longer repercussions (⤳⌐), and a figure
     with four regular notes (⋀) which, with the note before it, sings
     "fa–la–sol–la" —joy.

(5) One longer note (⌐) and three regular ones (⤳⋁), combining with
     the note before to sing "fa–sol–la" —joy.

(6) The note before *et* plus the two after it combine to make
     "fa–mi–sol–la"—the cross and resurrection.

(7) Two moderately longer notes (⋀) followed by two regular and two
     longer notes (⤳⌐).

(8) One long note (⌐), a quilisma followed by three longer notes
     (⤳⌐⌐), and two light notes (⋅⋅) leading into the next syllable. The
     first notes are "fa–sol–la–sol–la"—joy.

(9) One longer note plus three regular ones (⌐), possibly only two reg-
     ular notes according to St. Gall.

Mode VI: f–a

1 Corinthians: 5:7, 8 For even Christ our passover is sacrificed for us: Therefore let us keep the feast . . . with the unleavened bread of sincerity and truth.

Cantate Domino

Graduale Triplex–225   (Paschal time)

(1) 𝅘 𝅥   (2)
Can-<u>ta</u>-te <u>Do</u>-mi-no <u>can</u>-ti-cum <u>no</u>-vum, al-le-<u>lu</u>-ia; <u>qui</u>-a
  Sing   to Lord   song   new   who because

c   𝅘 𝅥   (3)
mi-ra-<u>bi</u>-li-a <u>fecit</u> <u>Do</u>-mi-nus, al-le-<u>lu</u>-ia; <u>an</u>-te con-<u>spec</u>-tum
 wonders has done Lord;   before   sight

(4) 𝅘 𝅥   c   c
<u>gen</u>-ti-um re-ve-<u>la</u>-vit iu-<u>sti</u>-ti-am <u>su</u>-am, al-le-<u>lu</u>-ia, al-le-<u>lu</u>-ia.
 of Gentiles has revealed   justice   his.

(1) The first note longer (⸝) followed by two regular notes, the second leaning into the third (𝅘).

(2) Two fast notes plus two longer ones, with a sign to "sing out" (𝆑).

(3) Four regular notes (ᵕ) plus three longer ones (𝆑).

(4) All eight notes moderately fast (,ᵉᵐ ⸝). (𝆑) means "joined."

Mode VI: f–a

Psalm 98 (97):1, 2   O sing unto the LORD a new song; for he hath done marvelous things. . . . His righteousness hath he openly shewed in the sight of the heathen.

IN. VI
RBCKS

C Antá-te Dó-mi- nō • cánti- cum no- vum, alle-

lú- ia : qui- a mi-ra- bí- li- a fe-cit Dó-mi- nus, alle-

lú- ia : • ante conspéctum gén-ti- um revē-lá-

vit iusti- ti- am su- am, alle- lú- ia, alle- lú- ia.

Viri Galilaei

Graduale Triplex–235 (Ascension)

                           C

V̱i-ri Ga-li-<u>lae</u>-i, quid ad-mi-<u>ra</u>-mi-ni as-pi-ci-<u>en</u>-tes in
Men of Galilee,   why   wonder   looking up   into

        (1) *S*   *ᴦ*

<u>cae</u>-lum? Al-le-<u>lu</u>-ia: Quem-<u>ad</u>-mo-dum vi-<u>di</u>-stis <u>e</u>-um
heaven?   Just as   you saw   him

           C   C C   *√* C   (2) *S*

a-scen-<u>den</u>-tem in <u>cae</u>-lum, i̱-ta v̱e-ni-et, al-le-<u>lu</u>-ia, al-le-<u>lu</u>-ia
ascending   to   heaven   thus he will come.

  (3) *S*

al-le-<u>lu</u>-ia.

(1) One longer note plus three regular (*ᴦ ѵ*).
(2) One longer note plus three regular (*ᐱ ѵ*).
(3) Three regular notes (*ѵ*) plus two regular and two longer
    notes (*ѵ≛*).

Mode VII: g–d

                                          CHANT MADE SIMPLE

Acts 1:11   Ye men of Galilee, why stand ye gazing up into heaven? this same Jesus . . . shall so come in like manner as ye have seen him go into heaven.

RBCKS **Antiphona ad introitum VII**

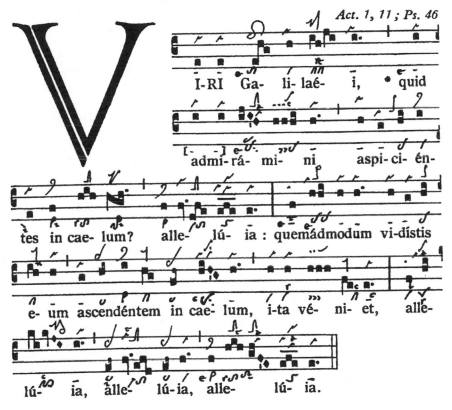

Act. 1, 11 ; Ps. 46

VI-RI Ga- li-laé- i, * quid admi- rá- mi- ni aspi-ci- én- tes in cae- lum? alle- lú- ia : quemádmodum vi-dístis e- um ascendéntem in cae- lum, i-ta vé- ni- et, alle- lú- ia, alle- lú-ia, alle- lú- ia.

Spiritus Domini

Graduale Triplex–252   (Pentecost)

⁽¹⁾ *π*   ⁽²⁾   *//*   ⁽³⁾ *ς*
Spi-ri-tus Do-mi-ni re-ple-vit orbem ter-rar-rum, al-le-lu-ia:
Spirit   of Lord   fills   whole   earth,

⁽⁴⁾   ⁽⁵⁾   *ʌ* ⁽⁶⁾ *J*
et hoc quod con-ti-net om-ni-a, sci-en-ti-am ha-bet vo-cis,
and that which   joins   everything   knowledge   has of languages.

⁽⁷⁾   ⁽⁸⁾   ⁽⁹⁾ *ς*
al-le-lu-ia, al-le-lu-ia, al-le-lu-ia.

(1) Two longer notes (*↙*) followed by three light notes (*·⁄*).
(2) The first note longer (*⌐*) plus two normal notes with the
    repercussion (*J*).
(3) A longer note (*↗*) followed by a three-note ornament (*ᴧ*).
(4) The caesura lengthens the second note (*J//*).
(5) Two longer notes (*⁄*) followed by three light ones (*·⁄*).
(6) Three light notes (*···*) leading into three longer notes (*ς*).
(7) Two light notes followed by three longer ones (*ᵕᴧᴐ*).
(8) Two light notes followed by three somewhat slower notes
    (*ᴧ ᵐᴧ*).
(9) A longer note (*↗*) followed by three regular notes (*ᴧ*).

Mode VIII: g–c

Wisdom 1:7 For the spirit of the LORD hath filled the whole earth: and that, which containeth all things, hath knowledge of the voice. (Douay-Rheims)

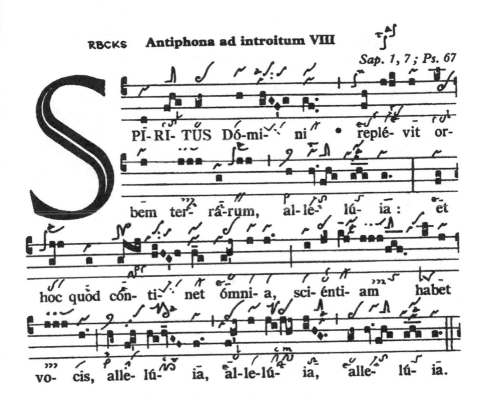

RBCKS **Antiphona ad introitum VIII**

Sap. 1, 7 ; Ps. 67

SPÍ-RI- TŮS Dó-mi- ni * replé- vit or-

bem ter- rá-rum, al-le- lú- ia : et

hoc quód cón- ti- net ómni- a, sci- énti- am habet

vo- cis, alle- lú- ia, al-le-lú- ia, alle- lú- ia.

Factus est repente

Graduale Triplex–256 (Pentecost)

(1)   T 𝄃
Fac-tus est re-pente de cae-lo so-nus ad-ve-ni-en-tis
Made   was suddenly from heaven sounds   happened

⌐   (2)   C   (3) C (4) 𝄃   (5)
spi-ri-tus ve-he-men-tis, u-bi e-rant se-den-tes, al-le-lu-ia:
breath   mighty   where   they were sitting

     C (6)   C   (7)
et re-ple-ti sunt om-nes Spi-ri-tu San-cto, lo-quen-tes
and filled   were all   with spirit holy   telling

     (8) C   (9) 𝄚
ma-gna-li-a De-i, al-le-lu-ia, al-le-lu-ia.
great things of God.

(1) A fast figure, perhaps suggesting "a mighty wind."
(2) Two longer notes (𝄃) followed by the liquescence (⌐) elid-
     ing the two *e*'s, the *h* being silent.
(3) A special torculus (♫), first note light followed by two longer
     ones.
(4) Two longer notes and two shorter ones (♪).
(5) One longer note followed by three regular ones (⟩∿).
(6) One longer note followed by two regular ones (⟩∿).
(7) Two short notes (♩) followed by three longer ones (♪).
(8) Three longer notes (⫽) followed by the salicus (⫶).
(9) One longer note followed by three regular ones (⟩∿).

Mode VII: g–d

Acts 2:2, 4 *Suddenly there came a sound from heaven as of a rushing mighty wind . . . where they were sitting. . . . And they were all filled with the Holy Spirit.*

CO. VII
RBCKS

Act. 2, 2. 4

F—Actus est re-pénte * de cae-lo so- nus adve-

ni- éntis spi-ri-tus ve-he-méntis, u-bi e- rant se-dén- tes,

alle- lú- ia : et replé- ti sunt omnes Spí-ri-tu Sancto,

loquén- tes magná- li- a De- i, alle-lú- ia,

alle- lú- ia.

Dicit Dominus

Graduale Triplex–263

✓ (1) ✓ (2) (3) (4) ⊼
Di-cit Do-mi-nus: Im-ple-te hy-dri-as a-qua et fer-te ar-chi-tri-cli-no.
Said   Lord: Fill   pots   water and take to steward.

  C (5) ⸜ (6) ⊼ T T   T ⸋ (7)
Cum gu-stas-set ar-chi-tri-cli-nus a-quam vi-num fac-tum, di-cit
When tasted   steward   water wine made   said

⸜ (8) ⊼ (9) ⊼
spon-so: Ser-vas-ti vi-num bo-num us-que ad-huc. Hoc si-gnum
to host : You saved wine good until now. This sign

fe-cit le-sus pri-mum co-ram di-sci-pu-lis su-is.
made Jesus first before disciples his.

(1) One longer note (⸝) plus three shorter (/.).
(2) Four longer notes (⸝⸝⊼).
(3) One longer note followed by the quilisma (⸝ ⸽).
(4) Two longer notes (✓) and three shorter ones (./).
(5) One longer note (⸝) followed by three regular ones (⸝).
(6) Two longer notes (⸝) followed by three shorter ones (./).
(7) Two longer notes (✓) followed by the salicus (⸋).
(8) Two longer notes followed by the quilisma (⊼ ⸽).
(9) Two longer notes (=) followed by three regular ones (ᴗ).

This chant could easily be thought of as a model for later oratorios and operas. It begins with a simple "recitative" by the narrator. Then Christ speaks (*Implete* . . .) in the low range always given to him at least through the classic era. When the narrator returns (*Cum gustasset* . . .) and tells about the steward tasting the wine, the melody weaves around over three notes, as if the steward had already had too much wine.

Then the steward breaks into a 3/4 dance figure in his tenor voice.

ser | -va - sti | vi- num | bo - | num | us - | que ad | - huc

And the whole thing ends with a simple chant by the narrator (*Hoc signum* . . .)

Mode VI: f–a–c

John 2:7–11 Jesus saith unto them, Fill the waterpots with water . . . and bear some of the water unto the governor of the feast. When the ruler of the feast had tasted the water that was made wine, . . . [he] saith unto [the bridegroom], . . . thou hast kept the good wine until now. . . . This beginning of miracles did Jesus . . . and his disciples believed on him.

Io. 2, 7. 8. 9 et 10-11

Omnes gentes

Graduale Triplex–297

⁽¹⁾   ⁽²⁾   //   ⁽³⁾   _S   ⁽⁴⁾   ⁽⁵⁾
<u>O</u>-mnes <u>gen</u>-tes <u>plau</u>-di-te <u>ma</u>-ni-bus: iu-bi-<u>la</u>-te <u>De</u>-o   in
All   people   clap   hands: shout   to God   with

    T   //
<u>vo</u>-ce ex-sul-ta-ti-<u>o</u>-nis.
voice   of triumph.

(1) Two regular, repercussed notes (//), three light notes (⸜), one regular and two longer notes (♪/) and three regular notes (⋀).

(2) One longer note (↗), two regular notes plus two longer notes (⌣ᵉ).

(3) Four light notes (⸜ᶠ).

(4) One longer note plus three regular ones (⌐ ⋀).

(5) Four longer notes (⸝ᵉ) plus five light notes (⸜ᵎ).

Mode VI: f–a

Psalm 47 (46):1   O clap your hands, all ye people; shout unto God with the voice of triumph.

Laetatus sum

Graduale Triplex–336

♪♪ (1) (2) ♩ (3) ♪ ♩
Lae-ta-tus sum in his quae dic-ta sunt mi-hi: in do-mum
Glad   I am in that which said was to me : into house

(4)ς
Do-mi-ni i-bi-mus.
of Lord   we shall go.

(1) One longer note (⌐), two light notes (⼂.), one longer note
(⁃), and three regular notes (⋎).

(2) One longer note (⼂), four light notes (⼂.), two regular notes
(⼂), and three longer notes (ς).

(3) One long note (⌐), two regular and one longer note (⋏),
two longer notes (⼃) and the rest regular.

(4) A long melisma on the first syllable: Two longer notes (♩),
two regular (⼂), two longer (⼃), three light (⼂.), a salicus (⼂), three longer notes followed by the quilisma (⼃⼃⋎),
leading to the next syllable.

Mode VII: g–d

Psalm 122 (121):1   I was glad when they said unto me, Let us go into the house of the LORD.

Amen dico vobis

Graduale Triplex–368

(1)
A-men di-co vo-bis, quid-quid o-ran-tes pe-ti-tis, cre-di-te
Amen   I say   to you,   whatever   desires   pray for,   believe

(2)   (3)   (4)   (5) ⌐
qui-a ac-ci-pi-e-tis, et fi-et   vo-bis.
that you   receive   and is done   for you.

(1) The caesura lengthens the second note (♪).
(2) Two longer notes (⁓), two regular notes (♪), and three shorter ones (·⁄).
(3) One longer note and three regular ones (⅄).
(4) Three longer notes (⁄⌐).
(5) A common cadence figure—two light notes leading to the longer top note (⁝), followed by three light notes (·⁄) leading into the final syllable (⌐).

Mode I: d–a

Mark 11: 24   Therefore I say unto you, What things soever ye desire, when ye pray, believe that ye receive them, and ye shall have them.

CO. I
RBAKS

A -men di-co vo- bis, * quidquid o-rántes pé- ti- tis,

cré- di-te qui- a acci-pi- é- tis, et fi- et vo- bis.

Qui manducat

Graduale Triplex–383 (Corpus Christi)

c ⸱⸱   (1)   ⸱⸱ π ⸍
Qui man-<u>du</u>-cat <u>car</u>-nem <u>me</u>-am, et <u>bi</u>-bit <u>san</u>-gui-nem
Who   eats   flesh   my,   and drinks   blood

(2)   (3) (4) π   π   (5)   ⸠
<u>me</u>-um, in me <u>ma</u>-net, et <u>e</u>-go in <u>e</u>-o, <u>di</u>-cit <u>Do</u>-mi-nus.
my   in me   lives   and I   in him,   says   Lord.

(1) Five-note, rather fast ornament (⸱⸍⸱).

(2) Another five-note, rather fast ornament (⸱⸍⸱).

(3) One longer note followed by the quilisma (⸗⸜⸍).

(4) Two longer notes (⸍) plus three shorter ones (⸱⸍).

(5) A melisma made up of one long note (⸗), two regular notes plus one long note (⸦⸍), two short notes (⸱⸱), two longer notes with a special sign not to hurry (x=expectare) (π⸱), and three regular notes leading to the final syllable.

Mode VI: f–a

John 6:56 He that eateth my flesh, and drinketh my blood, dwelleth in me, and I in him.

QUI mandú- cat carnem me- am, et bi- bit sán-
gui-nem me- um, in me ma- net, et é- go in
e- o, di- cit Dómi- nus.

BIBLIOGRAPHY

Graduale Triplex. Paris-Tournai: Abbaye Saint-Pierre de Solesmes & Desclée, 1979.

Gregorian Semiology. Dom Eugène Cardine (tr. Robert M. Fowells). Abbaye Saint-Pierre de Solesmes, 1982.

"Gregorian Semiology: The New Chant." Robert M. Fowells. In *Sacred Music*, Summer, Fall, and Winter, 1987.

If not available at your local dealer, the *Graduale Triplex* and *Gregorian Semiology* can be ordered directly from:

PARACLETE PRESS
P.O. Box 1568
Orleans MA 02653
800-451-5006
www.paracletepress.com